THANK GOODNESS FOR PEOPLE

Peanuts® Parade Paperbacks

THANK GOODNESS FOR PEOPLE

Cartoons from *Go Fly a Kite, Charlie Brown* and *Peanuts Every Sunday*

by Charles M. Schulz

Holt, Rinehart and Winston / New York

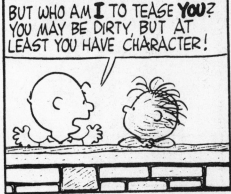

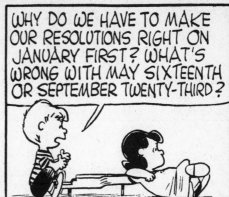

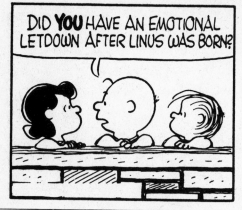

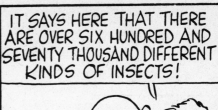

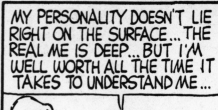

LINUS SAID THAT MISS OTHMAR REALLY SPOKE OUT AGAINST BLANKETS TODAY...

SHE SAID THAT IF A CHILD DRAGGED A BLANKET AROUND WITH HIM, IT WAS A SIGN OF IMMATURITY, AND SHE SAID THAT SHE WOULD NEVER PUT UP WITH THAT!

WOW!! THAT MEANS HE'S GOING TO HAVE TO CHOOSE BETWEEN HIS BLANKET AND MISS OTHMAR, DOESN'T IT?

WHO'S MISS OTHMAR?

SCHULZ

BUTTERFLIES LIKE ME!

SCHULZ

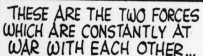

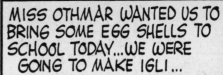

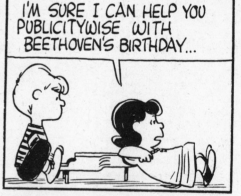

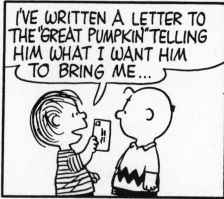

WHY DON'T WE GET THE WHOLE GANG TOGETHER, AND GO OUT AND SING PUMPKIN CAROLS?

...AND THEN ON HALLOWEEN NIGHT THE "GREAT PUMPKIN" RISES UP OUT OF THE PUMPKIN PATCH...

..AND HE BRINGS TOYS TO ALL THE GOOD LITTLE CHILDREN IN THE WORLD!

YOU'RE CRAZY!

ALL RIGHT, SO YOU BELIEVE IN SANTA CLAUS, AND I'LL BELIEVE IN THE "GREAT PUMPKIN"..

THE WAY I SEE IT, IT DOESN'T MATTER WHAT YOU BELIEVE JUST SO YOU'RE SINCERE!

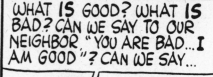

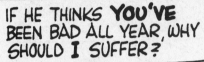

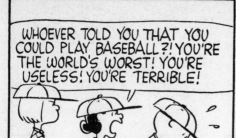

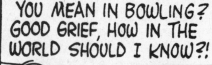

DEAR PENCIL-PAL,
    I GUESS BY THIS TIME
EVERYBODY BUT YOU KNOWS
THAT I HAVE A BABY
SISTER.

I SHOULD HAVE WRITTEN
SOONER TO TELL YOU, BUT
I HAVE BEEN VERY BUSY.
HER NAME IS SALLY. WE
LIKE HER AND SHE
LIKES US.

OH, OH!

IN A WAY, THIS HAS BEEN
A GOOD EXPERIENCE FOR ME.
I HAVE LEARNED A LOT.
                AS EVER,
                CHARLIE
                BROWN

SCHULZ

BEETHOVEN! ALWAYS BEETHOVEN!

I'LL BET BEETHOVEN REALLY WASN'T SO GREAT! I'LL BET HE DIDN'T EVEN HAVE ANY FRIENDS!

WHAT DO YOU MEAN, HE DIDN'T HAVE ANY FRIENDS?

JUST WHAT I SAID!

YOU NEVER READ ABOUT HIM PLAYING **GOLF** WITH HIS FRIENDS, DO YOU? **HUH**? DO YOU?! IF HE HAD SO MANY FRIENDS, WHY DIDN'T HE PLAY **GOLF** WITH THEM?

PEOPLE AREN'T FRIENDS UNLESS THEY PLAY **GOLF** TOGETHER! DID YOU EVER HEAR OF BEETHOVEN PLAYING GOLF WITH **HIS** FRIENDS? **NO, YOU DIDN'T!**

I CAN'T STAND IT! I JUST CAN'T STAND IT!

I WONDER IF LEONARD BERNSTEIN PLAYS GOLF WITH **HIS** FRIENDS?

CLOMP!

WEAK ANKLES!

SCHULZ

CLOMP

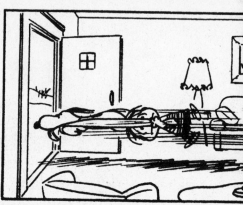

WHEW!

ARE YOU CRAZY? IT'S COLD OUTSIDE! YOU COULD CATCH PNEUMONIA ROLLING AROUND OUT THERE IN THE SNOW!

THE STRUGGLE FOR SECURITY KNOWS NO SEASON!

I SURE LIKE CHARLIE BROWN'S LITTLE SISTER..

SOMEHOW I FEEL THAT SHE AND I HAVE SOMETHING IN COMMON..

I JUST CAN'T FIGURE OUT WHAT IT IS, THOUGH...

THAT'S IT!

SHE'S THE ONLY OTHER ONE AROUND HERE WHO KNOWS HOW TO WALK ON FOUR FEET!

SCHULZ

LINUS! DON'T TELL ME YOU'RE RUNNING AWAY FROM HOME?!

YOU'RE CRAZY!! THEY KNOW YOU'RE BLUFFING! YOU'LL JUST MAKE A FOOL OUT OF YOURSELF!

YOU'LL HAVE TO GO BACK HOME THIS EVENING, AND THEN YOU'LL HAVE TO LISTEN TO YOUR MOTHER AND DAD TELL EVERYONE ABOUT HOW YOU TRIED TO RUN AWAY, AND YOU WERE SO CUTE AND SO SERIOUS AND THEY'LL ALL LAUGH!

IT JUST DOESN'T DO ANY GOOD! THEY'RE WAY AHEAD OF YOU!

!N OTHER WORDS YOU CAN'T FIGHT CITY HALL!

THAT'S RIGHT!

NOW, GO ON HOME, AND FORGET THE WHOLE THING..

❄WHEW❄ I WAS SCARED TO DEATH SOMEONE WASN'T GOING TO COME ALONG AND TALK ME OUT OF IT!

SCHULZ

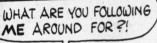

WHAT ARE YOU FOLLOWING **ME** AROUND FOR ?!

AM I SUPPOSED TO BE HONORED BY YOUR PRESENCE ?

GO ON! GET OUT OF HERE! WHAT MAKES YOU THINK EVERYBODY WANTS **YOU** AROUND ALL THE TIME ?!

SHE'S RIGHT...I MUST MAKE AN AWFUL NUISANCE OF MYSELF SOMETIMES...

SNOOPY!

OH, I'M SO **GLAD** TO SEE YOU! JUST KNOWING YOU'RE AROUND ALWAYS MAKES ME FEEL GOOD!

SCHULZ

BLAH

I CAN'T STAND IT!

LOOK AT 'EM·ALL LAUGHING AND ENJOYING THEMSELVES WITH THEIR VALENTINES!

I SENT EVERYONE I KNOW A VALENTINE, BUT DID I GET ANY IN RETURN? NO! NOT A SINGLE ONE!

EVERYBODY GETS VALENTINES EXCEPT ME! NOBODY LIKES ME!

LOOK AT 'EM! THEY ALL GOT VALENTINES! EVERYBODY GOT VALENTINES EXCEPT ME!

EVEN "PIG-PEN" GETS VALENTINES...

BUT DO I? NO!

I GET AS MANY VALENTINES AS A DOG!!

!

SIGH

SCHULZ

CLOMP

SCHULZ

HI.. **HI..**

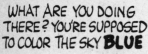

WHAT ARE YOU DOING THERE? YOU'RE SUPPOSED TO COLOR THE SKY **BLUE**

BLUE? THE SKY ISN'T **ALL** BLUE!

IT ISN'T?

THE SKY IS MANY COLORS..THERE'S A LITTLE BIT OF YELLOW THERE, SOME WHITE, SOME PINK, SOME GREEN AND..

YOU'RE CRAZY.

WELL, GO ON OUTSIDE, AND LOOK FOR YOURSELF!

ALL RIGHT, I WILL!!

WOULDN'T YOU SAY THE SKY IS BLUE, CHARLIE BROWN?

NO, I SHOULD SAY THE SKY IS MANY COLORS..THERE'S A LITTLE BIT OF YELLOW THERE, SOME WHITE, SOME PINK, SOME GREEN AND..

I OUGHTA SLUG YOU A GOOD ONE!

I DON'T EVEN KNOW WHAT'S GOING ON!!

I'LL PUT UP THE WICKETS, LINUS, AND YOU POUND IN THE STAKES...OKAY?

FINE.. I ALWAYS LIKE TO TACKLE A MAN'S JOB!

WHAP WAP WHAPPITY WHAP

POW POW POW

OH, GOOD GRIEF!

BOY, I'VE SEEN YOU LOOKING DEPRESSED, BUT I'VE NEVER SEEN YOU LOOKING **THIS** DEPRESSED!

I'M A RAT!

I FEEL TERRIBLE! I HATE MYSELF!!

I WAS SITTING ON THE FLOOR WORKING A PUZZLE, AND MY LITTLE BABY SISTER CAME CRAWLING OVER. SHE MESSED IT UP, AND I YELLED AT HER, AND SHE CRIED...AND I HATE MYSELF!

I SHOULDN'T HAVE YELLED AT HER...SHE'S ONLY A BABY...I FEEL TERRIBLE!

I UNDERSTAND WHAT YOU'RE GOING THROUGH, CHARLIE BROWN...DON'T FORGET THAT LINUS WAS A BABY ONCE, TOO...I HAD THE SAME PROBLEM...I USED TO FEEL THE SAME WAY THAT YOU DO...

HEY! IS THAT **MY COMIC BOOK** YOU'RE READING?

HOW MANY TIMES DO I HAVE TO TELL YOU TO LEAVE MY THINGS ALONE?!

IF I CATCH YOU WITH ANOTHER ONE OF MY COMIC BOOKS, I'LL CHASE YOU CLEAR OUT OF THE COUNTRY!

...BUT I GOT OVER IT!

OH, NO!

RATS! EVERY TIME YOU WANT TO DO SOMETHING, IT RAINS!

"RAIN, RAIN, GO AWAY... COME AGAIN SOME OTHER DAY!"

SLAM!

HIDE ME!

WHAT ARE YOU DOING, LINUS?

I'M MAKING MY OWN SET OF FLASHCARDS

THESE ARE JUST LIKE THE ONES THEY USE IN SCHOOL, AND THEY'RE A GREAT AID IN LEARNING TO READ..

I'LL HOLD THEM UP, CHARLIE BROWN, AND WE'LL SEE HOW GOOD A READER YOU ARE... READY?

LOOOK

UH HUH!

VERY GOOD...NOW TRY THE NEXT ONE..

TAYBUL

GOOD. AND THE NEXT?

KOW

VERY GOOD NOW LET'S GO A LITTLE FASTER..

PAYPUR, DORE, HOWSE, WELKUM, NIFE, SPUNE!

EXCELLENT! DO YOU WANT TO RUN THROUGH THEM AGAIN?

NO, I THINK ONCE IS ENOUGH...

AWL THYS REEDING IS HARRD ONN MI EYYS!

SCHULZ

BUT IS IT ART?

GOOD GRIEF, WHERE IS IT?

IF I EVER LOSE THAT BLANKET, I'LL CRACK UP FOR SURE!

WHERE'S THAT BLANKET OF MINE? I GOTTA HAVE THAT BLANKET..

HERE IT IS...HOT OUT OF THE DRYER!

WHOOP!!

WHOOP!

WHOOOP

WHOOP!

CLOMP

WHOOP

SCHULZ

SCHULZ

DON'T
BUG ME,
DOG!

✳ SIGH ✳

SCHROEDER, IF I TOLD YOU THAT I HAD THE FEELING YOU AND I WOULD GET MARRIED SOMEDAY, WOULD YOU CHUCKLE LIGHTLY OR LAUGH LOUD AND LONG?

I DON'T KNOW...IT'S KIND OF HARD TO SAY OFFHAND...

SCHROEDER, I HAVE THE FEELING THAT YOU AND I WILL GET MARRIED SOMEDAY...

HA HA HA HA HA HA

HO HO HO HO HA HA HA HA

HE'D LAUGH LOUD AND LONG!

THERE'S A LESSON TO BE LEARNED HERE SOMEWHERE, BUT I DON'T KNOW WHAT IT IS...

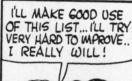

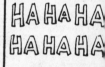

I'M GOING HOME TO EAT LUNCH, SNOOPY, AND I WANT YOU TO GUARD MY SNOWMAN.. DON'T LET ANYONE HARM IT!

ONE THING I'M GOOD AT IS GUARDING THINGS! IT'S A POINT OF DISTINCTION WITH MY PARTICULAR BREED!

I'LL GUARD THIS SNOWMAN AGAINST ENEMIES FROM THE NORTH, SOUTH, EAST AND WEST! I'LL GUARD THIS SNOWMAN AGAINST ENEMIES FROM BELOW AND FROM...

........above.........

YOU JUST CAN'T DO **ANYTHING**, CAN YOU?

..ANXIOUS CHILDREN WRITING THEIR LETTERS TO THE "GREAT PUMPKIN," GROUPS OF PEOPLE GETTING TOGETHER TO SING PUMPKIN CAROLS...IT'S WONDERFUL!

THERE'S SUCH A JOYOUS SPIRIT TO THIS SEASON!

YOU REALLY BELIEVE ALL OF THIS, DON'T YOU, LINUS?

WITH ALL MY HEART, CHARLIE BROWN..

I BELIEVE THAT ON HALLOWEEN NIGHT THE "GREAT PUMPKIN" RISES OUT OF THE PUMPKIN PATCH WITH HIS BIG BAG OF TOYS!

OH, WHAT A SIGHT THAT MUST BE TO BEHOLD!

THEN HE FLIES THROUGH THE AIR TO DELIVER THE TOYS TO ALL OF THE CHILDREN WHO HAVE BEEN GOOD

IF YOU'VE BEEN BAD DURING THE YEAR, YOU DON'T GET ANY TOYS!

THAT'S UNDER-STANDABLE

EXCUSE ME A MINUTE, CHARLIE BROWN..I WANT TO GO INTO THIS STORE..

THAT'S FUNNY..THEY SAID THEY DIDN'T HAVE ANY...IN FACT, THEY SAID THEY NEVER HEARD OF THEM...

NEVER HEARD OF WHAT?

PUMPKIN CARDS!

THAT'S VERY DISAPPOINTING...

I HAD PLANNED TO SPEND THIS EVENING ADDRESSING PUMPKIN CARDS!

SCHULZ

IF ANYONE HAD TOLD ME I'D BE OUT CRAWLING AROUND AMONG A BUNCH OF PUMPKINS ON HALLOWEEN NIGHT, I'D HAVE SAID THEY WERE CRAZY!

THIS IS FAR ENOUGH..

JUST THINK, CHARLIE BROWN... WHEN THE "GREAT PUMPKIN" RISES OUT OF THE PUMPKIN PATCH, WE'LL BE HERE TO SEE HIM!

IT JUST OCCURRED TO ME THAT THERE MUST BE TEN MILLION PUMPKIN PATCHES IN THIS COUNTRY.. WHAT MAKES YOU THINK WE'RE IN THE RIGHT ONE?

JUST A FEELING I HAVE, CHARLIE BROWN, ALTHOUGH I THINK THIS MUST BE THE KIND OF PUMPKIN PATCH HE WOULD PREFER...

I DOUBT IF HE LIKES LARGE PUMPKIN PATCHES...THEY'RE TOO COMMERCIAL..HE LIKES SMALL HOMEY ONES...THEY'RE MORE SINCERE...

SOMEHOW I'VE NEVER THOUGHT OF A PUMPKIN PATCH AS BEING SINCERE...

THERE HE IS! THERE HE IS!

IT'S THE 'GREAT PUMPKIN'! HE'S RISING UP OUT OF THE PUMPKIN PATCH

OHHH!

KLUNK

WHAT HAPPENED? DID I FAINT? WHAT DID HE LEAVE US? DID HE LEAVE US ANY TOYS?

NO TOYS... JUST A USED DOG...

HE MUST BE WELL ON HIS WAY BY THIS TIME.. HAPPY JOURNEY, O, GREAT PUMPKIN! HAPPY JOURNEY!

"USED DOG"! GOOD GRIEF!

SCHULZ

YOU KNOW, I CAN'T POSSIBLY TELL YOU HOW SICK I GET OF SEEING YOU DRAG AROUND THAT STUPID BLANKET!

IT'S NOT STUPID... THIS BLANKET HAS MANY VERY PRACTICAL USES...

HA! THAT'S A LAUGH!

YOU JUST HAVE NO IMAGINATION, THAT'S ALL

I HAVE PLENTY IMAGINATION... IT DOESN'T TAKE ANY IMAGINATION TO SEE HE'S CRAZY!

OF ALL THE BROTHERS IN THE WORLD, I HAD TO GET HIM!

WELL, YOU'LL HAVE TO ADMIT HE'S DONE IT AGAIN!

HUH?

I SAID LINUS HAS DONE IT AGAIN.. YOU'D BETTER GO SEE FOR YOURSELF...